★ IT'S MY STATE! ★
Hawaii

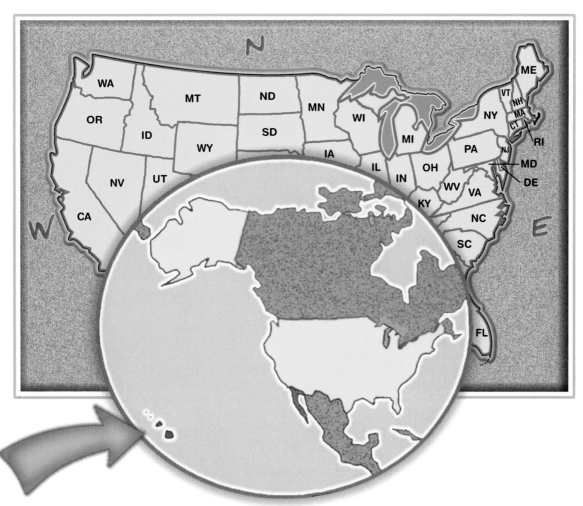

Ann Graham Gaines

 **Marshall Cavendish**
Benchmark
New York

Marshall Cavendish Benchmark
99 White Plains Road
Tarrytown, New York 10591-9001
www.marshallcavendish.us

Library of Congress Cataloging-in-Publication Data
Gaines, Ann.
Hawaii / by Ann Graham Gaines.
p. cm. — (It's my state!)
Summary: "Surveys the history, geography, economy, and people of
Hawaii"—Provided by publisher.
Includes bibliographical references and index.
ISBN-10: 0-7614-1926-8
1. Hawaii—Juvenile literature. I. Title. II. Series.
DU623.25.G35 2005
996.9—dc22
2005018060

Photo research by Candlepants, Inc.

Cover photograph: Joe Carini/The Image Works

Back cover illustration: The license plate shows Hawaii's postal abbreviation, followed by its year of statehood.

The photographs in this book are used by permission and through the courtesy of: *Corbis:* Douglas Peebles, 4 (middle) 12, 64, 74; Marc Muench, 4 (bottom); Robert Y. Ono, 8; Jim Sugar, 9; Frans Lanting, 11, 19; Michael T. Sedam, 13; Roger Ressmeyer, 14; Stuart Westmorland, 15; Richard A. Cooke, 21 (top); Bettmann, 22, 34, 36, 48 (middle), 48 (bottom), 35; Lucy Pemoni/Reuters, 27, 56, 69 (middle); Kelly-Mooney Photography, 37; Pete Saloutos/zefa, 38; Bob Krist, 47; Duomo, 49 (middle); Tim Wimborne/Reuters, 49 (bottom) David Sailors, 53; Mark E. Gibson, 55, 70; Elizabeth Kreutz/NewSport, 57; Richard Cummins, 58, 62; David Muench, 66; James L. Amos, 69 (top),71. *Photo Researchers Inc.:* Tom & Pat Leeson, 4 (top); Leslie Newman & Andrew Flowers, 5 (top); George D. Lepp, 16; Kevin Schafer, 20 (top); Michael Ord, 21 (middle). *Minden Pictures:* Flip Nicklin, 5 (middle); Chris Newbert, 20 (middle); Michael Durham, 20 (bottom). *The Image Works:* Joe Carini, 5 (bottom) , 40, 50; Jeff Greenberg, 45, 54; David R. Frazier, 68 (bottom); James Marshall, 72. *North Wind Picture Archive:* 26, 29, 33, 39 (top), 42, 48 (top), 49 (top). *Getty Images:* AFP, 43; 39 (bottom); Time Life Pictures, 51. *Animals Animals:* Leszczynski, Zigmund, 21 (bottom). *Envision:* Photononstop, 67; Dennis Galante, 68 (top); J.B. Marshall, 68 (middle); 69 (bottom).

Series design by Anahid Hamparian
Printed in Malaysia

1 3 5 6 4 2

Contents

A Quick Look at Hawaii

Nickname: The Aloha State

Population: 1,262,840 (2004 estimate)

Statehood: August 21, 1959

Bird: Nene

The nene (pronounced nay-nay), or Hawaiian goose, is a brown and gray goose that lives only in Hawaii. Unlike all other geese, the nene does not live near water. Instead, it lives on the slopes of the Mauna Kea and Mauna Loa volcanoes, on the Big Island of Hawaii.

Flower: Hibiscus

In 1988, Hawaii's state legislature declared the yellow hibiscus as the official state flower. Hibiscus flowers can come in a range of colors, including white, red, or pink. The striking flowers attract butterflies and hummingbirds.

Tree: Kukui

The kukui, or candlenut tree, was brought to Hawaii by the first Polynesian settlers. The tree's nuts, which are rich in oil, provided a source of light for the early Hawaiians. The nuts were placed in stone lamps and in torches and then lit. Other parts of the kukui tree were also used. For instance, kukui wood was used to build canoes, and the tree's inner bark was used to dye cloth. The kukui was chosen as Hawaii's official state tree in 1959.

Gem: Black Coral

Black coral are marine animals that live in colonies in tropical oceans. When many of these small animals grow together, their colonies look almost like trees. Black coral can be found in shady shallow water and deep down in underwater caves. Early Hawaiians harvested the skeletons of black coral to use as charms and to make medicine. Today black coral is often used in jewelry.

Marine Mammal: Humpback Whale

Female humpback whales, which are generally larger than males, can grow to be about 45 feet long. Every winter, thousands of humpback whales migrate from the icy waters off Alaska to the warm oceans around the Hawaiian Islands. Because so many humpbacks like to pass the winter months in the Hawaiian waters, a national marine sanctuary—which helps to protect the whales—has been established around each of the major Hawaiian Islands.

Dance: Hula

Hula has been performed in Hawaii since Polynesian people first came to the islands. Hula dancers honored their Hawaiian gods and rulers with their dances. Today, there are two different types of hula. Traditional hula dances are performed to chanted poetry and are often accompanied with the sounds of drumming. Modern hula dances are performed to music from steel guitars, ukuleles, and drums.

1 The Aloha State

The state of Hawaii is located in the middle of the Pacific Ocean. Located north of the equator, Hawaii is made up of an archipelago or chain of islands. Because it is surrounded by so much water, the Hawaiian archipelago is the most isolated land system on earth.

California lies about 2,380 miles to the east of Hawaii's capital city, Honolulu, while Japan is close to 4,000 miles to its west. In the past, it took weeks to reach these remote islands in a sailing ship. Today it takes tourists just a few hours to get to Hawaii by airplane. Many people think of Hawaii as a paradise because of its remote location and its incredible natural beauty.

A Chain of Islands

If you look at most maps of the state of Hawaii you will see only eight islands. In fact, the state covers the entire Hawaiian archipelago, which includes 132 islands, reefs, and shoals (sandy elevations), many of which are very tiny.

Because Hawaii is an island state, residents refer to the other states (not counting Alaska) as the mainland. To Hawaiians, the mainland includes the forty-eight contiguous, or connected, states on the North American continent.

Hawaii is far from being the world's largest archipelago, but it is still very long. The Hawaiian archipelago stretches over a distance of more than 1,500 miles. In terms of land area, Hawaii is made up of only 6,425 square miles, which makes it one of the smallest of all the states. But the state also includes another 4,500 square miles of water—found in the islands' many bays and inlets and in some of the surrounding ocean waters.

Hawaii's eight main islands are clustered at the southeastern end of the Hawaiian archipelago. They spread out over a distance of 350 miles. Going from the southeast to the northwest, they are Hawaii (also called the Big Island), Maui, Kahoolawe, Lanai, Molokai, Oahu, Kauai, and Niihau. People live on just seven of these eight islands since Kahoolawe is now abandoned. At one time, Kahoolawe was inhabited by a few

With its blue waters, sandy beaches, and interesting plants and wildlife, Hawaii is often viewed as a tropical paradise.

people, but during and after World War II, the small island was used by the American military as a place to practice bombing exercises. This practice ended in the early 1990s, but people still cannot live there.

In the early days, to get from one island to another, Hawaiians traveled by canoes. Today most people travel from one island to the other by airplanes, helicopters, or boats.

Volcanic Origins

The Hawaiian Islands are actually the tops of volcanoes. The bottoms of these volcanoes sit on the ocean floor. The land that lies above the waves is considered an island. According to geologists, the crust that forms the surface of the earth is broken into huge pieces called plates. These plates move very slowly.

Over the years, they bump together, causing earthquakes. Hawaii sits at the edge of a plate that many millions of years ago slowly passed over what scientists used to believe was a permanent "hot spot." At the hot spot, lava bubbled up through the crust of the earth and formed the Hawaiian volcanoes, one by one.

Kilauea has many active volcanic vents that can release molten lava. This is Puu Oo, Kilauea's easternmost vent. Kilauea is part of Hawaii Volcanoes National Park.

Slowly, the volcanoes moved off the hot spot and formed a long chain. The oldest volcanoes, at the northern end of the chain, have now sunk entirely beneath the waves. Others have sunk, but not all the way, and are now just reefs, with only the very tops of the volcanoes visible. Still others, like the active volcano Kilauea on the Big Island, remain high above the water. The very newest of the Hawaiian volcanoes—Loihi, which is located southeast of the Big Island—has not yet reached the ocean's surface.

In Hawaii, there are four volcanoes that have erupted in the past two hundred years. Today thousands of visitors go annually to see all four volcanoes. Three of them—Kilauea, Mauna Loa, and Hualalai—are on the Big Island. Haleakala, which is in Haleakala National Park, is on Maui. Haleakala is the world's largest dormant or inactive volcanic crater. Mauna Loa is the world's largest volcano. According to rangers at Hawaii Volcanoes National Park, Kilauea may be the most active volcano on earth. For most of the nineteenth century, Kilauea was erupting. Since 1952, it has erupted more than thirty times. Since 1983, there has been an area where the lava flow is active.

Hawaii is a record holder among the states. Ka Lae, a point on the south side of the island of Hawaii, is the southernmost point in the United States. Thanks to its many islands and shoals, Hawaii is the widest state. Hawaii is not, however, the westernmost point in United States. Alaska stretches farther out into the Pacific Ocean

The Islands, One by One

Each of Hawaii's main islands is different. The island of Hawaii is the biggest, which is how it got its nickname Big Island. Formed by five volcanoes, the Big Island still has two active volcanoes:

Mauna Loa and Kilauea. On the northern and southeastern coasts of the Big Island are very high cliffs, with waterfalls that flow into the ocean. The Big Island has the second-largest population of the islands, with close to 150,000 people. Still, it does not seem very crowded because the people are spread out.

Maui was formed by two volcanoes and has many canyons on its mountainsides. There is an isthmus (a narrow strip of land that connects the two volcanoes), where the soil is rich and sugar cane is easily grown. Maui is home to one of the world's largest banyan trees—it is so big that it covers a city block—and of the Needle, a monolith, or a mass of lava, that stands 2,250 feet high in the Iao Valley. Maui has a population of more than 130,000. Residents live in a few large towns and "upcountry," or out in a rural area where there are a few small villages.

Fog rises through Maui's coast, pushing through rock structures formed over millions of years.

The unpopulated island of Kahoolawe lies next to Maui. Until recently, it was used to test bombs The bombing left the island barren and dry. In order to make it beautiful once more, efforts are now underway to clean up the island and reintroduce native plants there.

For hundreds of years, the small and relatively wild island of Molokai was populated, like the other major islands in the chain. But in the 1860s, most of the healthy residents left because a leper colony was established there. Lepers are people who suffer from leprosy, a contagious disease that sometimes causes

The view from the cliffs on Molokai's north shore can be breathtaking.

body parts to fall off. Today the leper colony—though it is very small—still exists. But the island is also home to a population of around seven thousand people. Molokai attracts fewer tourists than other Hawaiian islands.

The small island of Lanai, which measures just 18 miles in length and 13 miles in width, is covered almost entirely by pineapple plantations. Like Molokai, Lanai has a small population, with just about three thousand residents. Most of them work for pineapple growers.

Oahu is the most populated island. There are a few stretches of wild coastline left on the island, but in other places it is almost entirely filled with businesses and homes. Oahu is known for its world-famous Waikiki Beach, a white sand beach that is lined with resorts and hotels. The state's capitol city of Honolulu, located on Oahu, has been described as one of the world's most exotic cities. It has both incredibly beautiful tropical landscapes and modern high-rise buildings.

Kauai has been described as a garden and is known for its amazing Waimea Canyon. This is a deep canyon 10 miles long and lined with exotic vegetation. The canyon was formed by rivers and floodwaters flowing down Mount Waialeale. This land mass is one of the wettest places on Earth and receives more rain than any other place. Many famous movies, including *Jurassic Park*, have been filmed on Kauai. The island has a population of roughly sixty thousand people, who live in the island's small towns.

Niihau is privately owned, so no one except the owners, their workers, and their guests see this island. Niihau has a population of 250 people, almost all of whom are of Polynesian descent. Hawaiian is the language spoken in most homes there.

Waimea Canyon on the island of Kauai is a striking sight to see. The canyon is nearly 3,000 feet deep.

A Natural Paradise

Even though some of the cities on the different islands are filled with modern buildings and crowds, the Hawaiian Islands still remain a place of astounding natural beauty. Surrounded by deep blue seas, all the

The United States can be divided into different time zones. Each zone covers many states. Unlike any other state, Hawaii has its own time zone.

islands have beautiful beaches. In some places, the sand on these beaches is white and sparkling. Other beaches are surprisingly made of black sand, which was formed when molten lava from a volcano poured into the ocean, cooled, and then eventually wore down into sand particles. Other portions of Hawaii's coastlines offer dramatically high cliffs.

This black sand beach is on the coast near one of Kilauea's active vents.

Hawaii's volcanic mountains all lie inland, and most of them are covered in thick tropical growth. Guava bushes, ferns, mango trees, and many more plants grow along the slopes.

Hawaii is home to several spectacularly different and fragile ecosystems. Ecosystems are natural areas in which living organisms—the plants and animals—interact. A rainforest is an example of an ecosystem. On Mauna Loa, there is a rainforest, where the jungle is thick and full of birds. On one side of Mauna Kea, on the other hand, there is a very different, dry forest. Very little rain falls on the area, which is perfect for plants like silversword—a low-growing plant that has clusters of pointed leaves and tall purple or red flowers—and other desert-like plants, such as cacti. The Hakalau Forest National Wildlife Refuge on the Big Island protects ohia and koa trees, which are very large. Especially interesting is the terrain around Kilauea, where lava flows often destroy the plants. Despite this, tiny new plants manage to push up through the lava and grow.

Hikers move through a fern forest in Hawaii Volcanoes National Park. The state's wet and warm climate is perfect for many plants not found on the mainland.

The Big Island is also home to the lush Waipio Valley. Other interesting features in Hawaii include the black volcanic rock and white sand found on the islands, as well as Molokai's and Kauai's unique red soil.

Although there are no large rivers or lakes in Hawaii, there are many beautiful small rivers and estuaries, which are aquatic habitats found at the mouths of rivers. Wailuku, which starts on the slopes of Mauna Kea on the Big Island, is the state's longest river. Kauai has several rivers, too, which are popular with many kayakers. Hawaii is also the location of some of the world's most beautiful waterfalls, some of which are very tall. Olo'upena Falls is the fourth-tallest waterfall in the

Waterfalls in Hawaii can be hidden in very interesting places. This waterfall is located in a red sand canyon in Kauai.

world. But many of Hawaii's waterfalls are hidden and hard to reach. Another interesting natural water phenomenon is called the blow-hole, where ocean waters spout up through lava tubes.

Mauna Kea is the tallest mountain in the world—when measured from its base at the ocean floor to its tip—with an elevation of 13,803 feet above sea level and another 18,000 feet below.

Hawaii's Climate

Hawaii's climate has been described as ideal. Although it can be humid, there are usually trade winds that bring cool air off the ocean. The highest temperature ever recorded in Hawaii was 96 degrees Fahrenheit. The weather is usually mild, averaging 72 degrees in places like Honolulu. In the winter, the temperature dips, but usually only into the sixties on the beaches. However, in the mountains temperatures can be very cold. While tourists bask in the warm winter sun at the beaches on the Big Island, they can look up at the crests of Mauna Kea and Mauna Loa and sometimes see snow.

Rainfall varies greatly over the islands. On the island of Hawaii, the small port of Kawaihae, located on the northwestern shore, typically gets only 8 or 9 inches of rain per year. But the city of Hilo, located on the eastern shore of the Big Island, gets more than 100 inches per year. On Kauai, Mount Waialeale—one of the wettest places on Earth—averages more than 400 inches of rain per year.

The forces of nature can be very strong in Hawaii. There have been many volcanic eruptions, earthquakes, hurricanes, flash floods, and even an occasional and disastrous tsunami, or tidal wave. Hilo was hit by these tidal waves in 1946 and 1960.

Hawaii's Plant Life

When many people think of trees in Hawaii, palm trees often come to mind. But there are so many other exotic trees that grow in Hawaii. One of these is the ohia, a very tall tree that grows on the volcanic slopes and is covered with red, yellow, or orange lehua flowers. The koa tree, which has a very hard red wood and can grow up to 100 feet tall, was used to make beautiful canoes in early times. Koa wood is also very popular for making furniture today. People in Hawaii are trying to encourage new growth of this popular tree. Other native trees include the guava and the banyan tree.

Plants Hawaiians grow for food include sugarcane, pineapples, papayas, bananas, mangoes, guavas, lichee, avocado, breadfruit, macadamia nut, lime, passion fruit, and tamarind. Other Hawaiian plants include tall tree ferns that grow in the rainforests. There are many different flowers that bloom all over Hawaii. Some of these flowers include orchids, anthuriums, and the sweet scented plumeria blossoms that are often used to make leis—strings of flowers that are worn on the head or placed around someone's neck.

Each of Hawaii's main islands has its own official flower. The kaunaoa is Lanai's. It is a yellow and orange plant that does not root in the soil, but gets nutrients from the air and rain. Its vines are picked and braided or woven together to form leis.

Animals in Hawaii

Before man came, there were only two types of mammals native to Hawaii—the hoary bat and the monk seal. There were also many kinds of lizards, insects, and birds. Offshore, a variety of fish, including marlin, dolphin, and tuna swam in the waters. Today six hundred species of fish have been identified as living in the Pacific Ocean off Hawaii.

When the islands' first inhabitants arrived, they brought with them dogs and pigs. By mistake, they also brought rats, which hid in their boats and canoes. Europeans brought cats, horses, cattle, goats, and sheep. In 1883, the mongoose—a small catlike mammal that eats meat—was introduced to Hawaii in the hopes that it would eat rats, which were ruining the sugarcane crop. However today Hawaii has serious problems with some of these introduced species, including the feral pig and the coqui frog. Feral or wild pigs are a problem because they eat important plants, which destroys birds' habitats. Coqui frogs compete with native species for food and homes. People also complain about the frogs because they make a lot of noise.

Because of loss of habitat, pollution, and other changes to the land and water, many species in the Hawaiian Islands are endangered. If nothing is done to help these animals and plants, they might disappear forever. Hawaii's residents, scientists, and lawmakers are working together to find ways to change this. Many acres of land have been set aside, and buildings, factories, or other structures cannot be built there. Laws have been passed to limit human contact with some endangered or threatened animals. Residents of the Aloha State are aware that the wildlife is an important part of their beautiful islands, and they will do what they can to protect it.

The long-legged Hawaiian Stilt walks through a marshy pond.

Plants & Animals

Monk Seal

Monk seals are one of two mammals native to Hawaii. Measuring up to 8 feet in length and weighing up to 600 pounds, monk seals are less social than other seals. In the ocean, monk seals dive deep—as much as 500 feet below the surface of the sea—to catch reef fish, lobsters, and octopus to eat. Today, only about 1,400 monk seals live on and off the Hawaiian Islands. They are endangered, partly because they often are harmed by dangerous trash like discarded fishing nets.

Green Sea Turtle

When baby green sea turtles hatch out of their eggs, their shells are only about 2 inches long. However, by the time they have grown up, their shells can be more than 2 feet long, and the turtles may weigh around 300 pounds. Scientists believe that some green sea turtles can live up to 80 years or more.

Hoary Bat

Hoary bats are forest dwellers that like to hunt over open land. Unlike many other bats, they do not live in colonies and instead roost or make their homes alone. Scientists fear that these bats may soon be extinct. But because the hoary bat is hard to catch or observe, scientists are not sure how many are left.

Ohia Tree

The ohia is a tree found on many of the different islands. Ohia trees produce a very beautiful red flower called the red lehua. A popular Hawaiian myth says that there was once a king named O'hia who so angered the goddess Pele, that she turned him into a tree.

Honeycreepers

There are many different kinds of honeycreeper birds living in Hawaii. Found in forests high on the mountains, the most interesting-looking honeycreepers are brightly colored and have curved bills. These bills are designed to help them drink nectar out of flowers. The tiwi, for example, is a brilliant red honeycreeper with a hooked bill. The tiwi lives in Ohia forests and feeds off the trees' flowers.

Triggerfish

Hawaiian waters—especially the coral reefs around the islands—are home to many different fish. Triggerfish are one type of reef fish. Different types of triggerfish have distinctive markings or colors. The humuhumunukunuku apua'a, or humuhumu for short, is commonly known as Hawaii's state fish.

2 From the Beginning

Hawaii was one of the last places on earth to be populated by people. Scientists believe Polynesians—people from islands in Asia—first arrived there sometime between 300 CE and 750 CE. For years Asians were traveling to and from the different islands in the Pacific Ocean. To get to many of these islands, they built huge sea-going canoes. Each canoe was big enough to hold dozens of people and to travel hundreds and thousands of miles. Because there were no maps and no landmarks to use in the middle of the ocean, travelers had to depend on signs to tell them where they were. These included ocean swells, currents, winds, and cloud formations. At night, they read the stars to find their way.

Experts believe that travelers—probably from the Marquesas, which were islands in the South Pacific Ocean—set out to find a new place to settle. These settlers might have been the first to arrive in the Hawaiian Islands. A second wave of settlement in Hawaii occurred around 1300 CE. These new people probably came from Tahiti. Others also traveled to make new settlements in the Hawaiian Islands from different islands in Asia.

Hawaiian natives rest outsides their straw hut in Honolulu around 1900.

Most of what is known of ancient Hawaiian history comes from stories told by the Hawaiian people. This form of storytelling is called an oral tradition. Many native Hawaiians know about their long-ago past because of stories and myths passed down from one generation to the next. Archaeologists—scientists who study ancient artifacts—are not able to add much information because weather and time have destroyed most of the islands' ancient buildings and artifacts.

Historians disagree about the origin of Hawaii's name. Some believe the islands were named after a fisherman named Hawaiiloa. Others think the name comes from Hawaiki, which was the former name of one of the Society Islands, where ancestors of Hawaiians might have lived. You may also see Hawaii spelled as Hawai'i. This spelling reflects the native Hawaiian language.

Chiefs and priests ruled each individual Hawaiian island a thousand years ago. But the islands were not united into a single kingdom. Chiefs claimed large plots of land as well as areas along the coast. They gave smaller portions of land to the rest of the people, for farming. Most people had to grow food not only to feed their families, but enough to also offer an annual tribute to their chief.

Religion was important to the early natives. Ancient Hawaiians worshipped Ku, the god of war. Many of the Hawaiian's other gods were of nature. Children grew up hearing legends of Pele, the goddess of the volcanoes, who Hawaiians believed demanded human

All ancient cultures had myths that helped people make sense of their world. Many of the Hawaiians' favorite myths center on Pele, the powerful goddess of volcanoes. As one story goes, Pele once became so angry with her youngest sister, Hi'iaka, she caused a huge volcanic eruption that destroyed Hi'iaka's favorite forest of Ohia trees.

Some artifacts and structures have survived through the years, giving scientists and historians clues to early life in Hawaii. These stones mark a sacred burial site made by early Hawaiian natives on Maui.

sacrifice. Public worship took place in a heiau, where there was an altar, a raised platform, and carved images.

Another things we know about ancient Hawaiians, despite the lack of written history, is that the arts were very important to them. They used wood, shell, stone, and bone in carvings and jewelry. They developed elaborate calendars that told them when to plant certain crops. Athletic contests were frequently held. Ancient Hawaiians went out in the ocean in canoes to fish and visit other islands, sometimes in order to trade and other times to fight.

For centuries Hawaiians have been building huge outrigger canoes capable of ocean-going voyages of hundreds—even thousands—of miles in length. Outrigger canoes have a main section where people sit. This section is carved out of wood. Attached to the sides of the canoes are outriggers, or logs, that keep the canoe balanced.

Captain Cook

In 1778, the first European ships landed at Waimea on Kauai. British Navy Captain James Cook, one of the most important explorers of his day, was their commander. Hawaiian myth stated that one day a new god would come from the sea. Many Hawaiians believed that Cook was this new god.

Captain Cook judged his first visit to Hawaii as a great success. His crews greatly enjoyed the time they spent on the islands, which were ruled by four chiefs. Cook described what he had named the Sandwich Islands as a tropical paradise. When he returned the next year for a second visit, however, trouble erupted. Cook and a few natives got into an argument over a boat the British believed the natives had stolen. Cook was killed and his crew fled to their ships and left the island.

Captain Cook recorded the name by which Hawaiians referred to their islands as Owhyhee.

Captain Cook and his crew dock in Kealakekua Bay. In 1779, however, this bay became the site of his death.

However, Cook's death did not end European interest in the islands. By this time, the British wanted to establish trade with China. One thing the Chinese wanted very much was to buy sandalwood, which grew in Hawaii at that time. Traders came to look for the sweet-smelling sandalwood. They would get the sandalwood from Hawaii and bring it back home to sell for a lot of money.

A New Kingdom

Around the time when Captain Cook first visited the islands, there was a young man named Kamehameha, who lived in Kohala on the northern shores of the Big Island. By 1790, he controlled most of the island. From there, he fought for control of more and more of the islands. By 1810 he had become Hawaii's first king, having united all the islands into a single kingdom.

A statue of King Kamehameha I stands in Honolulu. On an official holiday honoring the king, Hawaiians decorate his statue with leis made of native flowers and perform traditional dances and music.

Kamehameha I welcomed people from other countries such as Europe. He found them interesting and liked the goods they brought. Over time, Hawaiians became more and more accustomed to the foreigners. A few Hawaiians even agreed to leave Hawaii. In England and the United States, these Hawaiians created a great stir. Missionaries, people who traveled to new places to spread their religion, were interested in what they saw as a backward people. The missionaries began to talk of bringing the Christian religion to the islands.

In 1819, two important things happened. First, King Kamehameha I died and his wife ruled until one of his sons became old enough to be the new king. Also, American whaling ships arrived for the first time. With the arrival of the whalers, Hawaii's ports began to develop. The whaling ships came back to Hawaii every winter.

In 1820, after voyages that lasted many months, missionaries also arrived from New England. Over the years, fifteen different groups of missionaries came. Missionaries affected the lives of Hawaiian people in both bad and good ways. For instance, the missionaries forced Hawaiians to stop wearing their traditional clothing and to stop dancing the hula. But the missionaries also developed a written Hawaiian language and taught many native people to read and write.

One thing missionaries brought with them to the Hawaiian Islands was European and American education. Maui's Lahainaluna is the oldest high school west of Rockies. It was founded in 1831 by the missionaries.

Kamehameha's family remained in power for four more generations. Under the influence of the missionaries, King Kamehameha III developed a written constitution in 1840. For a long time, Great Britain, France, and the United

States all promised to leave Hawaii independent. But all of these countries wanted to possess the islands, especially after Hawaii began to play an important role in the world's economy. This came about after large crops of sugarcane were grown on the islands and exported to countries around the world.

By the 1870s, harbors like this one outside of Honolulu, were busy with European and American traders and whalers.

Tangram Puzzle Game

The fascinating puzzle called tangram originated in China. But Asian immigrants brought the puzzles with them to the Hawaiian Islands in the 1800s, where it soon became popular with Hawaiians of all ages.

What You Need

Stiff cardboard—at least 8 inches by 8 inches
Pencil
Ruler
Scissors
Poster paint

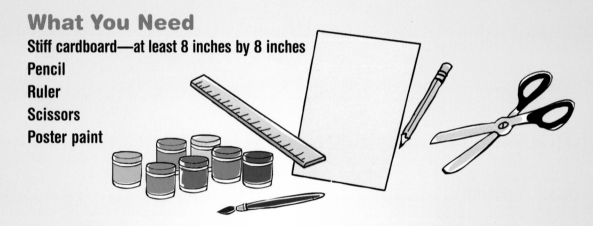

To make the tans:

With a pencil and ruler, mark an 8-inch square on the cardboard. Cut out the square.

Mark dots 2 inches apart along all four sides of the square. Connect the dots with light pencil lines to make a grid of sixteen squares.

Using this diagram as a reference, mark the five cutting lines on the grid. Make these lines dark enough so that you can see where to cut.

Cut along the five bold lines to create seven tans (shapes).

Spread newspaper on your work surface and paint the tans. When they are dry, you are ready to play.

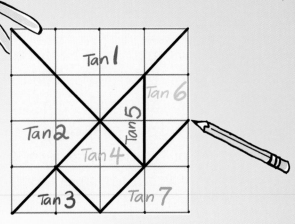

Instructions for the puzzle:

You have to arrange all seven pieces to make a shape—for example, a boat or an animal. All seven tans must be used.

To turn the puzzle into a game, have two players take turns, each making a shape that has not been done before. See who can make the most shapes, and have fun!

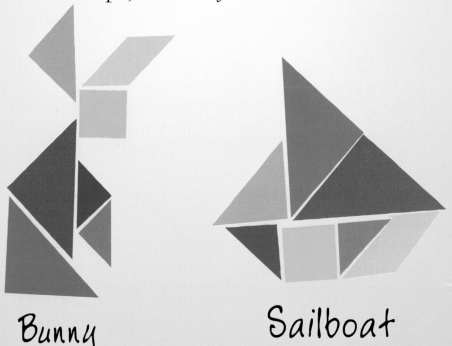

Bunny   Sailboat

In 1872, Kamehameha V died. In the years that followed, there were struggles over the throne. Some politicians wanted to ignore the natives' constitution. American influence in particular became greater and greater. This was especially true after businessmen like Sanford Dole established pineapple plantations on the islands. The businessmen wanted a great deal of say in how the islands were run.

In 1875 planters and other businessmen negotiated a special kind of treaty, called a reciprocity treaty, with the United States. This was a trade agreement that set out rules for trading and selling Hawaiian goods. The federal government said that Hawaii could sell sugar and other Hawaiian products in the United States without having to pay an extra tax to do so. Eventually, the United States was granted permission to build a naval base at Hawaii's Pearl Harbor. This gave the businessmen what they wanted, but only for a time. The businessmen then started to talk about annexation, which meant adding Hawaii to the United States.

But native Hawaiians did not want Hawaii to become part of the United States. They wanted to remain free and independent. In 1893, when Hawaiian Queen Lili'uokalani introduced a new constitution, Americans living in Hawaii—acting on their own ideas and not from any instructions from the United States government—overthrew her kingdom. They took away her power and started their own government in Hawaii. American President Grover Cleveland thought their actions were very unfair and demanded that Hawaii be given back to its people. But the businessmen who had taken over Hawaii ignored his wishes and formed a republic in 1894. Despite some American disapproval, the republic was officially recognized by the United States government.

These American men were part of the government of the Republic of Hawaii before the United States made the islands a territory in 1898.

In 1898, during the presidency of William McKinley, the Hawaiian Islands were annexed or added to the United States. Many native Hawaiians still did not want this, but the United States was too powerful and they could not stop the government. In 1900, the Hawaiian Islands were formally organized as a territory. (Throughout the history of the United States, new lands were often organized as territories before becoming states.)

Hawaii is the only state that was once an independent monarchy.

The Twentieth Century

In the opening decades of the twentieth century, Hawaiians began to realize they could make money and help their economy by attracting tourists to the islands. A tourist committee was formed for the first time in 1903. In 1915, the *Aloha Guide*—the first guidebook devoted to Hawaii—was published. The islands attracted tourists and new residents. In the years that followed, Hawaii's population grew very rapidly. In 1900, the territory had a population of approximately 150,000. By 1920, the number climbed to 255,881. The first luxury passenger ship docked in Hawaii in 1927. In 1935, mail was first carried across the Pacific—from California to the Philippines—with stops in Hawaii and other Pacific islands. Passenger flights to Hawaii soon followed.

By the 1930s, Hawaii's beaches were known as places to relax and have fun. Surfing became a popular sport among many visitors.

Growth of tourism was accompanied by the development of Hawaii for military bases. Hawaii has a very strategic location because it is the one of the only places in the middle of the Pacific Ocean where ships can safely dock for long periods of time. In the early 1900s, the U.S. Navy had built an important naval base at Pearl Harbor on Oahu.

Pearl Harbor would eventually become an important figure in World War II. On December 7, 1941, the Japanese attacked naval ships that were anchored in Pearl Harbor. This attack brought the United States into World War II.

Today Pearl Harbor is a popular place for many residents and tourists to visit. Memorials have been built to honor the many brave men and women who served on the base.

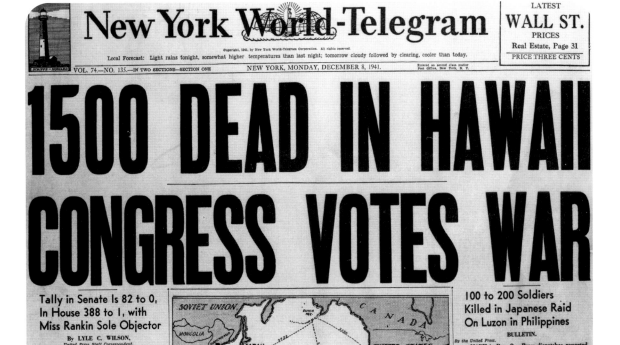

This headline ran in a newspaper on December 8, 1941—a day after the attack on Pearl Harbor.

During the war, Japan was the United States' enemy. Unfortunately, life became tough for Japanese immigrants or Japanese Americans living in the United States during the war. This was also true for Japanese Americans living in Hawaii. Even though

Even though many of their neighbors treated them poorly, many Japanese and Japanese-American residents of Hawaii signed up to help with the war effort.

most of them had nothing to do with the bombing and did not support Japan, they were discriminated against and treated poorly. Many of them were fired from their jobs and forced out of business. World War II eventually ended in 1945. But it was a while before Japanese Americans were treated as equal members of society.

After the war was over, Hawaii headed toward statehood. On August 21, 1959, President Eisenhower declared Hawaii the fiftieth state. This was an occasion celebrated by many Hawaiians,

Alaska and Hawaii were both admitted to the United States in 1959. Alaska became the forty-ninth state in January, but Hawaii did not join until August. As a result, the United States flag had forty-nine stars for only a very short time.

because now they would receive full representation in the federal government. They felt that their voices could be heard and they would receive the same benefits from the United States government that all states receive.

Tourists visiting Hawaii in the 1980s look up to see these naturally-hanging ferns in Kauai.

Waikiki Beach on Oahu is a popular spot for residents and tourists alike.

In the 1960s and the decades that followed, Hawaii saw more and more changes as tourism increased and the state's economy strengthened. Things changed again, however, in 1995 when Asia's economy became troubled. Up until that point, many tourists had come every year to Hawaii from Asia. But the number decreased greatly. Tourism fell off even more sharply after September 11, 2001, because many people became afraid to fly, due to the threat of terrorism.

However, people have begun to travel once more in greater numbers, many of them making Hawaii their destination. The state's economy has started to recover, though things are not as prosperous as they once were. But Hawaiians are a tough people, who have withstood many struggles and hardships. There is no doubt that this great state will continue to forge ahead into the future, with residents prepared to face whatever comes their way.

Important Dates

300 – 750 CE The first Polynesians arrive in Hawaii.

1000 – 1300 A second wave of settlers comes from Tahiti.

1627 Spanish sailors report that they see a volcano erupt in the Pacific. Some people believe they have seen Hawaii.

1778 Captain James Cook and his ships' crew arrive at the islands by chance.

1810 King Kamehameha I unifies his kingdom of islands.

1820 American missionaries arrive.

1840 Hawaiians write their first constitution.

1875 The kingdom of Hawaii enters into a reciprocity treaty with the United States.

1885 Japanese contract laborers come to work on Hawaii's sugar plantations.

1893 Queen Lili'uokalani is overthrown.

1894 The Republic of Hawaii is established.

1898 The United States annexes Hawaii.

1900 Hawaii is organized as a territory.

1941 On December 7, the Japanese attack Pearl Harbor, bringing the United States into World War II.

1959 On August 21, Hawaii is officially admitted into the Union as a state.

1978 The state's constitution sets up an Office of Hawaiian Affairs to provide help for native Hawaiians.

1992 Hurricane Iniki hits Kauai.

1993 The United States Congress passes a resolution apologizing to native Hawaiians for the time when American citizens living in Hawaii overthrew the kingdom.

2002 Linda Lingle takes office as Hawaii's first female governor.

Captain Cook

Linda Lingle

3 The People

Based on its population, Hawaii is ranked forty-second among the fifty states. In 2004, there were about 1,262,840 people living in Hawaii. Most of the people, around 800,000, live on Oahu in the capital city of Honolulu.

People from Many Lands

Back in the days before Captain Cook came to the islands, the only people who lived in Hawaii were of Polynesian descent. After Cook died and traders started to visit, a few Europeans came to live on the islands.

In 1789, an American trader sailed to Hawaii. His crew included many Chinese sailors. Some of them jumped ship, apparently deciding they would rather live in paradise than keep living a hard life on the seas. More and more Chinese people came, especially between 1850 and 1898.

The first American missionaries arrived from the United States in 1820. In the years that followed, the population of

The Hawaiian Islands' first residents were most likely from Polynesia. Many Hawaiian traditions practiced today come from Polynesian customs.

Hawaiian natives perform their traditional dances and music for Europeans and Americans who just arrived on the islands.

Americans living in Hawaii grew steadily. Many of them were missionaries, but people in other lines of work—including merchants, craftsmen, and writers—came, too. When sugarcane and pineapple plantations were developed on the islands, Asians—including Chinese, Japanese, and Filipinos (people from the Philippines)—were brought over in large numbers to work in the fields. The lives of these people were extremely hard. Many worked for cruel bosses for almost no money. Nevertheless, many of these people stayed on in Hawaii, sending for their relatives, and starting families who would help Hawaii grow.

Today, Hawaii differs from the other forty-nine states because there is no ethnic majority. In other words, no single ethnic group makes up more than half of the population. The largest group is of Asian descent. Asians make up just over 40 percent of the population. Caucasians—or white people—make up one quarter of the population. Native Hawaiians and people from other Pacific Islands make up approximately 10 percent of the population. The Hispanic population has recently grown and now makes up about 7 percent of the population. Many Hispanic people living in Hawaii were originally from Puerto Rico or are of Puerto Rican descent. Only 2 percent of the people who live in Hawaii are African American. One-third of 1 percent (or .3 percent) are Native American. With all of this diversity, it is no surprise that many Hawaiians are of mixed heritage. Around 20 percent of Hawaiians are

Hawaii's ethnic makeup is different from most other states. This is mostly because of the islands' location in the Pacific Ocean.

descended from two or more races.

Many Hawaiian residents are from other states. Some Americans come to enjoy the tropical weather all year long. Others move to Hawaii to retire or start new island-related businesses.

There have long been cowboys in Hawaii. Explorer George Vancouver brought cattle to the islands in the 1790s. One of the biggest cattle ranches in the United States can be found on the Big Island.

Polynesian Influence

One of the things that makes visiting Hawaii especially interesting is seeing the many ways in which there is still a great deal of Polynesian influence. Today, there are not very many native Hawaiians left—these are the people who are directly descended from the first residents. Yet many of their ways have been adopted. Many people on the islands like to wear brightly colored and loose fitting clothing. Hawaiian shirts—which are usually brightly colored and decorated with bright designs—are very popular. Women also occasionally wear muumuus, which are long dresses decorated with flowers or patterns. Missionaries encouraged the natives to first put these on, because they objected to the clothing that the natives wore. During festivals and other celebrations, many Hawaiian women wear traditional clothing, such as grass skirts. Leis, which are necklaces made of flowers, shells, or feathers, are a popular symbol of Hawaii. Natives and visitors often wear these pretty ornaments.

Hawaiians' diets resembles other Americans' in many ways. But Hawaiians tend to eat more fruit, just like early

These Hawaiian girls are making traditional leis to be worn during dance performances at a luau.

Hawaiians, because it is so plentiful on the islands. Many of the state's residents also like to eat traditional food such as poi. Poi is a dish made from the pounded and cooked root of the taro plant, which grows on the islands. To celebrate birthdays and other special occasions, many people in Hawaii hold luaus, or feasts, in which the featured dish is usually a roasted pig.

Hawaiian Angela Perez Baraquio, who is of Filipino descent, wowed millions of television viewers when she danced the hula during the talent portion of the Miss America competition in 2001. She went on to win the crown.

Other elements of traditional Hawaiian culture that have survived include music and dance. Hawaiian music features instruments including the ukulele, slack key guitar, and drums. The hula is often performed to entertain residents and visitors and also to honor the state's native history.

In Hawaii, there is a special pidgin language spoken by many that combines English slang with Hawaiian words.

The Hawaiian language is also still very much alive. Many people speak the language fluently. Those people who do not speak Hawaiian still know many words in this language. Many people use the word *aloha* as a greeting and call tourists *malihini,* a word that means "newcomer." Other popular words that are used are *kai,* which refers to the sea, and *mauna,* which means "mountain."

Sometimes traditional Hawaiian foods include a mix of Chinese, Filipino, Japanese, or Polynesian recipes.

Famous Hawaiians

Father Damien: Missionary

Born in Belgium as Joseph de Veuster, he adopted the name Father Damien when he traveled to Honolulu and became a priest. In the 1870s, he went to Molokai to minister to the hundreds of lepers who had been sent there to live in isolation. Father Damien improved their lives in many ways, including helping them to plant trees and build a water system and houses. Father Damien eventually died from leprosy he caught from the patients on Molokai.

James Dole: Businessman

American James Drummond Dole was the first businessman to make a fortune selling pineapples. Arriving in Hawaii in 1899, he established his first pineapple plantation on Oahu. In the 1920s, he bought the entire island of Lanai so he could grow pineapples there. The original Dole cannery closed in 1991, but Hawaiian farms that grow fruit for Dole are still thriving.

Duke Kahanamoku: Athlete

During his teenage years, Duke Kahanamoku spent a lot of time at the beach riding 16-foot surf boards carved out of koa wood. In 1911, he and his friends formed one of the very first surf clubs. In 1912, he competed as a swimmer in the Olympics, breaking the world record in the 100-meter freestyle race. Later in life, he became an actor and served as sheriff of Honolulu. Kahanamoku died in 1968.

Lili'uokalani: Queen

Queen Lili'uokalani—also known as Lydia Kamakaeha—became queen in 1891. Two years later, Americans living in Hawaii took away the queen's authority. She was kept under house arrest for eight months and in 1895, she gave up her claim to the throne. Afterward, she spent a lot of time in the United States fighting in court for compensation for the land that was taken by the Americans. Queen Lili'uokalani died in 1917. In Hawaii, she is remembered not only as a beautiful queen, but also as an accomplished songwriter and a very generous spirit.

Michelle Wie: Athlete

Born in Hawaii in 1989, Michelle Wie started to play golf when she was four years old. At the age of ten, she became the youngest person ever to qualify for a USGA (United States Golf Association) amateur championship. In 2002, she became the youngest girl to play an LPGA (Ladies Professional Golf Association) Tour Event. Sportswriters expect Wie—who, at age fourteen, already stands over six feet tall—to one day compete with the men in their professional championships.

Bette Midler: Actress and Entertainer

Bette Midler was born and raised in Honolulu. While enrolled at the University of Hawaii, she landed a small part in the movie and then moved to Los Angeles and New York to pursue her career. Midler has starred in many movies, has performed many sold-out concerts, and has many best-selling albums.

Asian Influence

Hawaii is home to many people who came from Asia. They brought their own customs, languages, and religions. In Honolulu, there is a large Chinatown where Chinese, Vietnamese, Laotian, Japanese, Thai, Filipino, and Korean people have shops and restaurants. These markets and restaurants can also be found in various places on the different islands. People come to the markets to buy special Asian products and foods, including rice noodles and duck eggs.

Recently, historians have been collecting information about the history of Asian people in Hawaii. They have been trying to document, for example, the very hard life that Asian workers led on pineapple plantations. Oral history projects

A young Hawaiian is dressed in traditional Japanese clothing for a parade celebrating Asian heritage in Hawaii.

Despite the fact that they did very hard work for long hours, many plantation workers were not paid a lot and had trouble providing for their families. These three boys were the children of Filipino field workers who lived in Hawaii in the 1940s.

collect people's stories, like that of Japanese-born Tsuru Yamauchi, who moved to Hawaii as a young woman of twenty. She told an interviewer what it was like to work on a plantation in the early twentieth century: "We moved to #10 Camp. I cooked and washed clothes there [for] about 8 years. . . . I did laundry for others. At that time we had to wash everything by hand, scoop and carry the water from the faucet to the bathhouse. . . . Oh, I sure did everything. And as for ironing, it was charcoal iron. We put in two pieces of charcoal and adjusted the heat until it got warm. I got paid $1 a month per person. I did cooking, washing, everything. I got only one dollar. That is all."

> *"Hawai'i, Hawai'i*
> *Like a dream so I came*
> *But my tears are flowing now*
> *In the canefields."*
>
> **—This is an example of a Japanese "*Hole hole bushi*," a folk song that described life and work among immigrant laborers on Hawaii's sugar plantations.**

Asians, Asian Americans, and other Hawaiian residents are all a part of the state's history. Through their hard work and determination, the state grew and prospered.

Life in the Big City

According to the federal government, today almost 900,000 Hawaiians live in a city or in the suburbs around a city. That is close to three quarters of the state's population.

> **Hawaii has more sumo wrestlers than any other state. (Sumo is a traditional Japanese sport.) A Hawaiian, Chad Rowan, was the first non-Japanese sumo wrestler to win the sumo wrestling championship.**

Many feel that Hawaii has just one very large city, its capital, Honolulu. It has a population of about 370,000. Honolulu is a city of contrasts, where tropical beaches, picturesque historic buildings and gleaming, modern high-rises are found. Many businesses are based in Honolulu, providing jobs for its citizens. As the largest city, Honolulu also attracts many tourists. The money these tourists spend in the city helps the local economy. The city has beautiful parks and beaches, but many of Honolulu's residents also complain about the city's terrible traffic congestion, as well as the growing air and water pollution.

During the day, Waikiki Beach's white sand and brilliant blue waters dominate the landscape. At night, however, the city lights shine brightly for residents and visitors who go to the city to enjoy themselves.

Life Away from the Big City

Hawaii does have other cities, but they are all much smaller. They include Hilo, Kane'ohe, Kailua, Pearl City, Kahului, and Kailua-Kona.

Hilo, on the eastern shores of the Big Island, is the second-largest city in Hawaii. It has just a little more than one-tenth of Honolulu's population, with approximately 40,000 residents. Kane'ohe and Pearl City (both on Oahu) and Kahului (on Maui) have more than 20,000 people. Kailua-Kona, on the sunny side of the Big Island, does not even have 10,000 residents. There are still many Hawaiians who live in small villages where there is little more than a

Hawaii today has been shaped by the many different people who have made the islands their home throughout the years.

school, a church, a small grocery store, and a post office. In many of these places, people live in old Hawaii-style frame houses with tin roofs. Many of these houses are leftover from the time when plantations were very important in the islands.

People who live on Oahu enjoy many of the attractions of big cities—they shop at huge malls and go to different museums, concerts, and theaters. The other islands are just as modern—with schools, malls, and other attractions. But there are not as many, and the cities are not as crowded. Many feel that life on the less-populated islands moves at a slower pace. Unfortunately, there are often fewer jobs available in some of the other islands, but residents find a way to make it work.

But no matter where people live in Hawaii, everyone can enjoy the natural beauty of the islands. No one is ever far from the shadow of a mountain, and most people live close enough to the ocean that they can walk or ride their bikes to a beach. Wherever they come from and wherever they live, Hawaiian residents are happy to call the state their home.

Hawaii has the lowest unemployment rate in the country. That means that Hawaii has fewer people without jobs than any other state.

Snorkeling off of one Hawaii's many beaches is fun for residents and visitors of all ages.

Calendar of Events

Narcissus Festival

Held on Oahu in January, the Narcissus Festival, which lasts for five weeks, is part of the Hawaiian Chinese community's New Year celebrations.

Whale Day Celebration

Humpbacks are celebrated at Kalama Park, on Maui, one Saturday every February. People go there not just to learn about the whales, but to eat, drink, buy arts and crafts, and take part in games and a parade.

Prince Kuhio Day

March 26 marks Prince Kuhio Day, an official Hawaiian state holiday. It honors Prince Kuhio, who served the Hawaiian territory as its first delegate to the United States Congress from 1903 to 1922.

Merrie Monarch Days

For forty years, the Hawaii Island Chamber of Commerce has sponsored the Merrie Monarch Days on the Big Island in April. The highlight is a three-day hula competition. Dancers start to prepare months in advance, taking lessons, attending seminars, and practicing.

Lei Day

On Lei Day, the first of May, many people in the Hawaiian Islands wear the traditional garlands of flowers or shells. There are lei-making competitions and a Lei Queen is crowned.

A Japanese Lantern Ceremony

Celebration of Canoes

People come from many different Pacific nations to take part in Maui's annual celebration of canoes. At this May event, you can see canoes being carved or watch canoe races.

Pan Pacific Festival-Matsuri in Hawaii

In June at this festival on Oahu, people from Hawaii and Japan get together for many different kinds of cultural events. This includes music, art, theater, dance, and food.

Makawao Rodeo

Held on Maui, this is the largest rodeo held in Hawaii. This July event features traditional rodeo events, including roping bulls, rodeo clowns, and western music.

Ukulele Festival

The world's best ukulele players—up to three hundred of them—get together in July to play at the Ukulele Festival. This festival, celebrating the little guitarlike instrument, is held in Waikiki.

Ironman Triathalon Competition

Every October, athletes come from around the world to the Big Island to compete in this seventeen-hour race. The race requires participants to swim in the ocean, bike for 112 miles, and run a marathon.

Kona Coffee Festival

The Kona Coffee Festival, held on the Big Island, lasts for two weeks in November. It includes many events celebrating not only Hawaii's coffee, but its growers and their diverse backgrounds.

The Ironman World Championship

4 How It Works

In some ways, Hawaii is similar to other states. Hawaiians are represented in the federal government by two senators and two representatives in Congress. Like other United States citizens, Hawaiians vote for the president every four years. Hawaii also has a state government that works for everybody who lives on the islands.

Daniel K. Inouye, the first Japanese American ever to serve in the U.S. Congress, has been one of the senators from Hawaii since 1963. His political career started when he was elected to the U.S. House of Representatives in 1959, as the state's first congressman. Born and raised in Honolulu, Inouye is also a decorated war veteran who lost his arm during World War II. Inouye is highly respected in the senate and has worked hard to represent his home state.

The Judiciary Building in Honolulu is sometimes called the Old Courthouse because it was used as the government capitol when Hawaii was a kingdom and a republic. Today, part of the building is a museum dedicated to the history of Hawaii's governments.

In other ways, Hawaii's government is unlike any other state's. At the local level, Hawaii has only county governments. Many other states have city and town governments in addition to county governments. County governments in Hawaii take on all the responsibilities usually held by city or town governments. For example, county governments are in charge of fire and emergency medical services, police forces, trash pickup, and street maintenance.

Today Hawaii has four counties. There used to be a fifth, called Kalawao County, which covered the leper colony of Molokai, but it now is part of Maui County. It can be challenging to be part of a county government in Hawaii because some counties include more than one island. In Hawaii, it is the counties rather than the cities that have a mayor. For example, one person is mayor of the county of Honolulu, which covers the island of Oahu. This includes the city of Honolulu, plus thousands of mostly unnamed islets and reefs which do not have any people living on them.

Honolulu has the longest borders of any city in the world. The state constitution says that any island (or islet) belongs to Honolulu if it does not belong to a county. As a result, Honolulu is about 1,500 miles long or about as long as half the distance across the forty-eight states on the mainland.

Hawaii is also remarkable because it has only one public school district for the entire state. All the other states have many school systems, but Hawaii has only one. The state's board of education has fourteen members. One nonvoting member is a student.

State Government

Honolulu is Hawaii's state capital. Most of the state's government offices are located there. Because Hawaii is such a new

Branches of Government

Exceecutive The executive branch enforces laws. This branch includes the governor, lieutenant governor, and state agencies, such as the office of the attorney general.

Legislative This branch makes state laws. Hawaii's legislature includes a state senate and a house of representatives. The house of representatives has fifty-one members. The senate has twenty-five members. Legislators' terms are two years long and there is no limit to how many terms a legislator can serve. The legislature meets every year from January through May.

Judicial Hawaii's Supreme Court reviews laws to see if they are fair and do not go against the state constitution. When a court case is decided but is appealed, it is the Court of Appeals that reviews the case to see if it was handled fairly or if a mistake was made. Like many states, Hawaii also has district courts, trial courts, family courts, and other small courts.

state, it has not had very many governors. When Linda Lingle became governor of Hawaii in 2002, she became the sixth elected governor. She is also the first woman to be governor of Hawaii. In the past, the governor of the state lived in Queen Lili'uokalani's mansion, called Washington Place. But the mansion is being turned into a museum and a new house—called the Governor's Residence—has been built.

From Bill to Law

It takes many steps for a bill to become a law in Hawaii. First, a legislator—a state senator or member of the house of representatives—and his or her staff must draft a bill and have it introduced and assigned a number. After being read, the bill is referred to a committee. The committee can choose to change it, pass it, or reject it. Bills that make it through committees are read for a second and third time on the floor, where they can also be debated by members of the legislature or senate, depending on where the bill was introduced. Once the bill is passed—approved by a vote—it is sent to the house or the senate, whichever chamber has yet to discuss it. There, it is debated again.

State legislators meet at the capitol building in Honolulu.

Once both houses pass a bill, it goes to the governor. The governor can sign the bill into law or veto—reject—it. If the governor vetoes a bill, it can still pass if the house and senate overturn the governor's veto. In order to do this, two-thirds of both houses must vote to override the veto. If this happens, then the bill becomes a law.

Getting Involved

Hawaiians have many opportunities to get involved in their government. Some people run for election and then fill a political office. Others volunteer their time. Many more people make their voices heard by contacting their representatives to tell them how they feel about an issue or how they want their representatives to vote on a specific bill. Anyone can call or write to their representatives' offices.

Hawaii has an unusual state capitol building, which was opened in 1969. On the first floor are the state senate and the house chambers where the legislators meet. These chambers are shaped like cones to symbolize volcanoes. (The offices in the building, however, do not have an unusual shape.)

Many ideas for bills have actually come from Hawaiian residents. Over the years, residents of Hawaii have organized many times to bring about positive change. One thing they worked for was to stop the bombing on Kahoolawe. Hawaiians have also tried to get the government to protect 'alala, or Hawaiian crow, and to make the humuhumu the state's official fish. From local issues to state issues, everyone can make a difference.

To contact Hawaii's state legislators, go to this Web site: http://www.capitol.hawaii.gov. Click on "House" or "Senate" to find contact information.

5 Making a Living

Before explorers and missionaries came to the islands, Hawaiians had a subsistence economy. In other words, they did not make things to sell to other people. Families took care of themselves, growing and making enough for what they needed.

By 1800, ships were coming to Hawaii to trade. They anchored off Lahaina, on the island of Maui, where they loaded their ships with sandalwood. American whalers came every year to the north Pacific Ocean, searching for the sperm whales, which they killed for their blubber. Whale blubber was processed into oil, which was used as fuel for lamps. On their way to the north Pacific, the captains of whaling ships often went to Hawaiian ports to pick up supplies and to allow their sailors to enjoy some time on the shore. In 1849, after California's Gold Rush went into full swing, sailing ships on their way to the west coast of North America also frequently stopped in Hawaii.

Americans and Europeans first bought land in Hawaii in order to grow sugarcane. Hawaii is an ideal place to raise sugarcane because it is a crop that needs rich soil and a great deal

An aerial view of farms and palm trees in Maui. Agriculture is not the most profitable industry in Hawaii, but many residents manage to make a living on their farms.

of rain. Sugarcane is processed and made into sugar and other goods. Pineapple plantations were also set up to take advantage of the warm, wet weather.

Agriculture Today

For a long time, agriculture formed the backbone of the Hawaiian economy. This changed, however, in the twentieth century when Hawaiians began to make more money from tourism and the military.

Smooth-shell macadamia trees were introduced to the islands in the 1800s. Since then, Hawaii has been well-known for these delicious nuts.

Today the state's largest ranches and plantations are almost all owned by corporations. There are only 5,500 family farms. Some crops are grown on a small scale and are sold to local grocery stores and restaurants. These include beans, corn, lettuce, potatoes, tomatoes, and taro, a plant grown for its root. Farms raise cattle, dairy cows, and hogs. They also produce eggs for the residents and tourists on the islands to eat. Crops grown for export (to be sent out to other places) include sugarcane, pineapples, flowers—especially orchids, coffee, macadamia nuts, avocados, bananas, guavas, papayas, and other fruits.

A taro plantation on Kaui provides the state—and places outside of Hawaii—with taro roots for cooking.

Recipe for Coconut Haupia

In Hawaii, coconuts are used for a variety of foods and drinks. Follow these instructions to make this tasty coconut dessert. Haupia is often served at traditional luaus in Hawaii.

Ingredients:

Coconut milk (12 ounce can, which can be
   found in most grocery stores)

1-1/2 cup water

1/2 cup sugar

6 tablespoons cornstarch

1/4 teaspoon vanilla

Have an adult help you with the stove.

Pour the coconut milk and water into a saucepan on the stove. Set the stove to low heat. Slowly add all the other ingredients into the pan. Keep stirring until the mixture thickens like a pudding. Be careful not to cook the mixture for too long or it will get burned.

When it is well mixed and thick, pour the haupia into an 8 x 8 baking pan and put it in the refrigerator.

When it is cool, it will be stiffer than regular pudding. You will be able to cut it into squares and serve it to your friends and family. Enjoy this tropical treat!

Products & Resources

Sugar

The first successful sugarcane plantation in Hawaii began operations in 1834. Sugarcane is a grass plant that contains a sweet juice that is processed to become sucrose or sugar. In 1959, one out of every twelve workers in Hawaii was involved in the sugar industry. There are still sugarcane plantations in Hawaii, though the crop is not the moneymaker it once was.

Pineapple

The pineapple plant is low-growing and takes a long time to produce a fruit. For decades, Hawaii had many pineapple plantations. Pineapples are no longer grown in huge numbers on the islands, but there are still thriving plantations. These farms employ a large number of Hawaiians, even though machines make it easier to harvest the fruit.

Cattle

Hawaii is home to many beef cows that eat the islands' rich grasses. But ranchers have had trouble making a great deal of money from their beef, because they cannot afford to bring in the grain cows also like to eat. The cost of shipping the cattle long distances can also sometimes be a problem for ranchers. Still, Hawaii beef is an important state product.

Orchids

Orchids are showy flowers—and many smell sweet. Hawaii's tropical climate is ideal for these plants. Many orchids grow wild in Hawaii's natural areas. But they are also specially grown on farms or in green-houses to be sold to the rest of the United States, Europe, and Asia.

Military Bases

Another huge source of money for Hawaii is the federal government. This is because of the many military bases that exist in the state. The United States Navy first became interested in building a naval base at Pearl Harbor in the 1840s. The Army, Air Force, and Marines also have bases in Hawaii. The government has also estab-lished very important satellite tracking facilities in the state. All of these military facilities provide jobs for Hawaiian residents who serve the military or are civilians—non-military people.

Coffee

Coffee is made from a bean that grows on an evergreen tree. Farmers say it is the year-round warm weather, the rich vol-canic soil, and the light winds and rain that make Hawaiian coffee special. Hawaii is the only state that grows coffee and Kona is the most famous of all Hawaiian coffees.

Pacific Waters

Some Hawaiians make their living from the water. Many tourists love to sport fish in Hawaii. Charter boat operators make a lot of money taking people out to fish in the Pacific Ocean. Snorkeling and scuba diving are also popular. Instructors and stores that rent equipment to tourists can profit from Hawaii's waters.

A few hundred Hawaiians also make their living today catching fish. Swordfish and big-eye tuna bring in the most money. Today there is also some aquaculture around the islands. This involves growing animals and plants in the water. Some people involved in aquaculture raise algae, which are microscopic plants that fish and other small aquatic animals like to eat. Others raise shellfish, such as shrimp.

Special filters and pumps are used on this algae cultivation plant in Kailua-Kona on the Big Island.

Manufacturing

Manufacturing has never been very important in Hawaii. Other than food-packaging plants, there are not a lot of factories. But manufacturing does provide a living for some Hawaiians. The state's leading manufacturing activity is food processing. Food processing plants prepare and package food made from crops and animals grown on the islands.

There are also, however, some traditional goods that Hawaiians make and sell to other states or other countries. Hawaii is often associated with the ukulele. An early version of this little guitarlike instrument was first brought to the islands by Portuguese immigrants who arrived in the 1800s. Hawaiians grew to love the instrument and became well known for their skills at playing and making them. There are several family-owned ukulele makers in Hawaii.

The ukulele's name has to do with the way it is played. To play the instrument a person needs to move his or her fingers quickly up and down the strings. *Uku* in Hawaiian means "flea," and locals thought that the ukulele players' fast-moving fingers were like a flea jumping around.

A group of schoolchildren perform with their ukuleles.

Though factories in other states or countries make ukuleles, many musicians and collectors prefer to get their instruments from the Aloha State.

Tourism

Hawaii makes most of its money from tourism. Most visitors come from the United States, although Hawaii is also a very popular destination for people from Asia. For many Americans, Hawaii is a great getaway, where they can relax on tropical islands without actually leaving the United States.

Hikers enjoy the canyons in Kauai's Koke'e Park. People looking for a fun outdoor trip have a lot of choices on Hawaii's many islands.

The wildlife in Hawaii is unlike anywhere else on the mainland. Many visitors enjoy hiking through the forest, seeing the volcanoes, snorkeling or scuba diving along the reefs, or simply relaxing on the beach. The different cultural events and the historic sites are also popular among tourists.

Tourism helps Hawaii's income in many ways. Many Hawaiian residents are employed by hotels, resorts, restaurants, museums, or stores where visitors spend their money. And every time a new hotel is built to house more tourists, people in the construction industry are able to find new jobs and earn money.

Tourists arriving in Hawaii are often greeted with leis made of flowers, nuts, leaves, or shells.

Hawaii's Future

Today Hawaii has economic problems that its leaders and people are trying to take care of. After September 11, some people became afraid to travel, especially by airplane. This meant that fewer tourists came to Hawaii and businesses were hit hard. And when the economy of the the United States— and that of the rest of the world—is not doing well, tourism to Hawaii will slow down some more. This will make it very hard for residents to find jobs. Some may decide to move to the mainland for different opportunities.

Prices for many different goods are always going to be very high in Hawaii because most goods have to be transported there through ship or airplane. For example, a gallon of milk in Hawaii often costs twice as much as a gallon of milk on the mainland. This is not because milk had to be brought over from the mainland, but because grain for the islands' cows costs a lot of money.

But there have been some good changes in Hawaii's economy. For example, lately there are more and more jobs in healthcare on the islands. This could attract health professionals who would like to live on the islands. The leaders of Hawaii have promised to work very hard to try to create new jobs for Hawaiians. The state especially wants to encourage growth in science and technology, film and television production, sports, ocean research and development, health and education, tourism, different forms of agriculture, and floral and specialty food products that can only come from Hawaii. Hawaiians have had to deal with tough times before. And together the state residents are committed to finding ways to keep the Aloha State's economy alive and well.

Local schoolchildren perform traditional dances for tourists visiting Honolulu. Whether it is for the amazing landscape, the interesting history, or the native traditions, visitors will always find Hawaii to be a welcoming place.

Hawaii

Hawaii's flag has the Union Jack—the flag of Great Britain—in its upper left-hand corner. The Union Jack appears because British explorer George Vancouver gave the British flag as a gift to King Kamehameha I. At the time, Kamehameha was bringing together the islands, and decided to use the Union Jack as Hawaii's unofficial flag. Eventually, eight red, white, and blue, stripes were added to symbolize the eight islands.

In the center of the seal is a design based on the old royal coat of arms of the Kingdom of Hawaii. King Kamehameha I is shown holding a staff, and the Goddess of Liberty is holding a flag. The seal also has many symbols, including a tabu ball and stick which stand for the power of the government. The seal also features eight taro leaves, a phoenix, and a star. The top of the seal has the words State of Hawaii and the year the state joined the union. The state's motto is on the bottom.

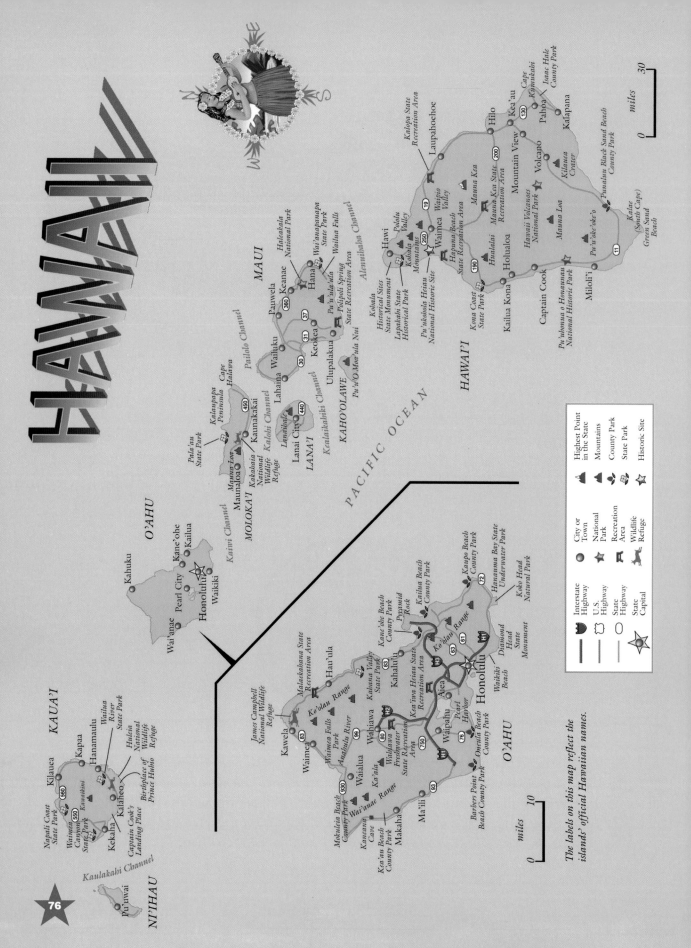

HAWAII

NI'IHAU

Pu'uwai

Kaulakahi Channel

KAUA'I

Napali Coast
State Park

Kilauea

Kapaa

Hanamaulu

Wailua
River
State Park

Waimea
Canyon
State Park

560

550

Kawaikini

Kekaha

Kalaheo

Huleia
National Wildlife
Refuge

Captain Cook's
Landing Place

Birthplace of
Prince Kuhio

O'AHU

Kahuku

Kane'ohe

Kailua

Pearl City

Wai'anae

Honolulu

Waikiki

Kaiwi Channel

MOLOKA'I

Kalaupapa
Peninsula

Cape
Halawa

Pala'au
State Park

Mauna Loa

Maunaloa

Kaunakakai

450

Kakahaia
National
Wildlife
Refuge

Kaloni Channel

LANA'I

Lana'i City

Lanaihale

440

Kealaikahiki Channel

KAHO'OLAWE

Pu'u O Moa'ula Nui

Pailolo Channel

MAUI

Haleakala
National Park

Wai'anapanapa
State Park

Wailua Falls

Hana

Pu'u'ula'ula

Polipoli Spring
State Recreation Area

Keanae

360

Pauwela

Wailuku

37

Keokea

31

30

Lahaina

Ulupalakua

Waihee

Alenuihaha Channel

PACIFIC OCEAN

Kohala
Historical Sites
State Monument

Lapakahi State
Historical Park

Pu'ukohola Heiau
National Historic Site

Kalopa State
Recreation Area

Laupahochoe

Hilo

Kea'au

130

Pahoa

Isaac Hale
County Park

Cape
Kumukahi

Kalapana

Hawi

Pololu
Valley

Kohala
Mountains

250

Waimea

Hapuna Beach
State Recreation Area

19

Waipio
Valley

Mauna Kea State
Recreation Area

200

Mountain View

Volcano

Kilauea
Crater

Punalu'u Black Sand Beach
County Park

Mauna Kea

Hualalai

Holualoa

190

Hawaii Volcanoes
National Park

Mauna Loa

Pu'u 'oke'o

Kalae
(South Cape)
Green Sand
Beach

Kona Coast
State Park

Kailua Kona

Captain Cook

Pu'uhonua o Honaunau
National Historic Park

Miloli'i

11

HAWAI'I

O'AHU

Kaupo Beach
County Park

Kailua Beach
County Park

Pyramid
Rock

Kane'ohe Beach
County Park

Hanauma Bay State
Underwater Park

72

Ko'olau Range

61

Koko Head
Natural Park

Diamond
Head
State
Monument

63

Waikiki
Beach

H1

Honolulu

Malaekahana State
Recreation Area

Hau'ula

Kahaluu

Kahana Valley
State Park

83

Ke'aiwa Heiau State
Recreation Area

Aica

Pearl
Harbor

H3

H2

Wahiawa

Kawela

Ko'olau Range

Kahuku Valley
State Park

Waimea
River

99

Wahiawa
Freshwater
State Recreation
Area

80

76

750

Waipahu

Oneula Beach
County Park

James Campbell
National Wildlife
Refuge

Waialua

Ka'ala

930

Mokuleia Beach
County Park

Waimea Falls
Park

Kanana
Cave

Wai'anae Range

Makaha

Ma'ili

93

Barbers Point
Beach County Park

Kea'au Beach
County Park

The labels on this map reflect the
islands' official Hawaiian names.

0   10
miles

0   30
miles

Legend

🛣️	Interstate Highway
🛡️	U.S. Highway
⬭	State Highway
⬭	State Capital
●	City or Town
★	National Park
⛺	Recreation Area
⬟	Wildlife Refuge
◤	Highest Point in the State
◤	Mountains
🌿	County Park
✿	State Park
✦	Historic Site

Hawaii Ponoi

Words by King David Kalakaua
Music by Henry Berger

Ha - wai - i po - no i, Na - na i kou mo - i
Ha - wai - i's own true sons, Be loy - al to your chief,

Ka - la - ni A - li - i, ke A - li - i.
Your coun - try's liege and lord, The A - li - i.

CHORUS

Ma - ku - a la - ni e Ka - me - ha - me - ha e
Fa - ther a - bove us all, Ka - me - ha - me - ha e,

Na kua - a e pa - le Me ka i - he.
Who guard - ed in the war With his i - he.

More About Hawaii

Books

Doak, Robin. *Hawaii the Aloha State*. Milwaukee, WI: World Almanac Library, 2003.

Heinrichs, Ann. *Hawai'i*. Minneapolis, MN: Compass Point Books, 2004.

Liitschwager, David, and Susan Middleton. *Remains of a Rainbow: Rare Plants and Animals of Hawai'i*. Washington, D.C.: National Geographic Society, 2001.

Web Sites

Hawai'i's Official State Web Site
http://www.hawaii.gov/portal

Hawai'i Visitors and Convention Bureau
http://www.gohawaii.com

Virtually Hawaii
http://satftp.soest.hawaii.edu/space/hawaii/index.html

About the Author

Ann Graham Gaines lives with her children deep in the woods of Texas. For close to twenty years, she has been writing children's nonfiction books and doing picture research. Every year she dreams of Hawaii: in January, when the icy winds blow off the plains, and in August, when the Texas heat seems like it will never end.

Index

Page numbers in **boldface** are illustrations.